W9-AYY-451

NATIONAL GEOGRAPHIC INVESTIGATES NATIONAL GEOGRAPHIC INVESTIGATES NATIONAL GEOGRAPHIC INVESTIGATES NATIONAL GEOGRAPHIC INVESTIGATES NATIONAL GEOGRAPHIC INVESTIGATES NATIONAL GEOGRAPHIC INVESTIGATES NATIONAL GEOGRAPHIC INVESTIGATES NATIONAL GEOGRAPHIC INVESTIGATES NATIONAL GEOGRAPHIC INVESTIGATES NATIONAL GEOGRAPHIC INVESTIGATES NATIONAL GEOGRAPHIC INVESTIGATES NATIONAL GEOGRAPHIC INVESTIGATES NATIONAL

Ancient
Africa

Archaeology Unlocks the
Secrets of Africa's Past

WITHDRAWN

Ancient Africa

Archaeology Unlocks the Secrets of Africa's Past

By Victoria Sherrow

James Denbow, Consultant

PORTER MEMORIAL BRANCH LIBRARY
NEWTON COUNTY LIBRARY SYSTEM
6191 HIGHWAY 212
COVINGTON, GA 30016

NATIONAL
GEOGRAPHIC
Washington, DC

Contents

< The ruins of the Great Mosque in Kilwa, Tanzania. Kilwa was a major trading port on
the East African coast. The mosque dates from the 13th century A.D.

◀ Huntsmen gather under an acacia tree in Shaba Game Reserve, Kenya. They carry
spears and shields similar to those used by their ancestors for thousands of years.

From the Consultant

Africa is one of the largest and most diverse continents on Earth, so it is perhaps not surprising that the origins of all humankind trace back to it. It now appears that fully modern humans also have their origin in Africa.

But that is only the beginning of the fascination of Africa's past. Ancient Egypt and its neighbor Nubia are among the earliest civilizations on Earth, predating ancient Greece and Rome by almost 2,000 years! By the first centuries A.D., Africans were part of trade networks that spanned half the globe— north across the Sahara to the Mediterranean and east across the Indian Ocean as far as Indonesia and even China. The continent has contributed its peoples, its ideas, and its goods to world events time and time again. Echoing the words of the famous Roman writer Pliny the Elder, "There is always something new out of Africa."

I hope this book will provide at least a starting point to encourage readers to dig deeper into the amazing richness and diversity of Africa's past.

James Denbow
2006

James Denbow (right) with colleagues at the archaeological site of Toutswemogala in eastern Botswana.

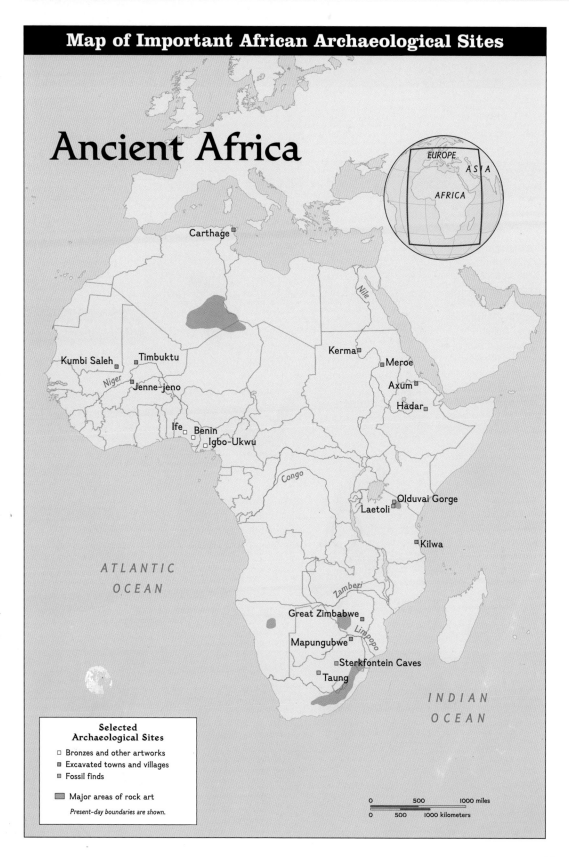

Map of Important African Archaeological Sites

Ancient Africa

EUROPE
ASIA
AFRICA

Carthage

Nile

Kumbi Saleh   Timbuktu   Kerma
         Niger   Meroe
              Jenne-jeno   Axum
                                                 Hadar
           Ife   Benin
                  Igbo-Ukwu

                          Congo

                                        Olduvai Gorge
                              Laetoli

                                          Kilwa

ATLANTIC
OCEAN

                          Zambezi

              Great Zimbabwe
                          Limpopo
          Mapungubwe
                    Sterkfontein Caves
              Taung
                                       INDIAN
                                       OCEAN

Selected
Archaeological Sites

□ Bronzes and other artworks
▣ Excavated towns and villages
▢ Fossil finds

▨ Major areas of rock art

Present-day boundaries are shown.

0   500   1000 miles
0   500   1000 kilometers

9

FOUR MAJOR PERIODS OF
African History

Early humans

**4 MILLION YRS B.C. –
ca 160,000 YRS B.C.**

Fossil remains of hominids (members of the same family as modern humans) dating back more than four million years have been found in southern and eastern Africa.

The oldest fossil remains are of the line called Australopithecus. There are several different species of Australopithecus. One of them may have developed into the Homo line from which modern humans are descended.

The earliest remains of modern humans have also been found in Africa. These fossils date back at least 160,000 years.

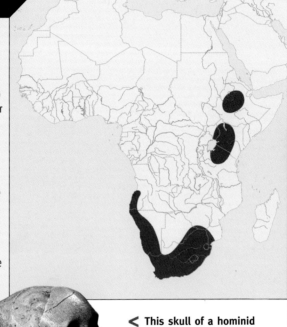

< This skull of a hominid child is about 1.7 million years old. It was found near Taung, South Africa.

Ancient kingdoms

3100 B.C. – A.D. 325

The fertile Nile Valley saw the rise of the ancient civilizations of Egypt and Nubia (Kush) beginning in the fourth millennium B.C.

> This Nubian pot comes from the city of Kerma in Sudan.

Timeline of African History

	8000	7000	6000	5000	4000	3000	2000

PREHISTORY

4 million years B.C. Early hominids lived in East and southern Africa
2.5 million years B.C. Stone tools made at Hadar, Ethiopia
160,000 B.C. Modern humans lived in East and southern Africa
10,000 B.C. End of the last ice age: the Sahara becomes a grassland

ca 7500 B.C. First Saharan pottery

ca 8500 B.C. First Saharan rock art

ca 6500 B.C. Domestication of cattle in the Sahara

ca 6000 B.C. Domestication of plants in the Sahara; sheep, barley, and wheat introduced to Egypt from Middle East

ca 3100 B.C. Egypt becomes a state

ca 2530 B.C. Construction of Great Pyramid at Giza in Egypt

ca 750 B.C. Phoenician settlement built at Carthage

East African traders

A.D. 800 – 1500

In the ninth century, trade began to increase along the east coast as Arab traders made contact. Trading towns such as Manda and Kilwa were established. In the interior, complex societies began to develop. They were linked to the coastal region by a trade network. But they also grew wealthy through cattle-rearing and metalworking.

V This terra-cotta head from the Nok culture of Nigeria dates from between 500 B.C. and A.D. 200.

West African kingdoms

A.D. 500 – 1591

The first millennium A.D. saw the rise of powerful cities, states, and empires in West Africa. Their wealth was based on trade. The earliest was the Ghana empire, which flourished from around A.D. 500. It was well located to take advantage of the trade routes between North Africa and the gold-producing areas to the south. From the ninth century, trans-Saharan trade increased. Arabs traded salt for ivory, ebony, gold, and slaves. Powerful states included Mali, Songhay, and Kanem-Bornu.

B.C. 0 A.D. .... **500** .... **1000** .... **1500** **2000**

a 100 B.C. Camels re introduced nto the Sahara, which helps evelop trans-aharan trade

ca A.D. 325 Axumites destroy Nubian capital Meroe

ca A.D. 500 Bantu peoples reach southern Africa with iron and cattle

ca A.D. 641 Arabs conquer Egypt and spread into North Africa

ca A.D. 750 Growth in trans-Saharan trade between North and West Africa

ca A.D. 800 Merchants settle and trade along East African coast

ca A.D. 1250 Stone Central Enclosure built at Great Zimbabwe

ca A.D. 1520 Trans-Atlantic slave trade begins

1807 Slave trade abolished in British Empire
1869 Suez Canal opens
1870s European countries compete to colonize Africa in the "Scramble for Africa"
1957 Ghana is first African colony to gain independence from European rule

MODERN ERA

11

Yesterday Comes Alive

CHAPTER 1

How do we learn what we know about the past?

Who were the first humans? Where did they live? When did they start making tools? What did they eat? How did they build communities? What beliefs guided them? Some of these questions may never be answered. But experts have learned much about people who lived before history was written down. In this book, you will look for answers, too, as you join archaeologists at work in Africa. Africa was once called the Dark Continent by Europeans who knew little about it. Of course, Africa was never isolated from world events, and today the clues it provides are shedding

< These Nubian pyramids in Sudan were built between 300 B.C. and A.D. 300, more than 2,000 years after pharaohs stopped building royal pyramids in Egypt.

light on some of the earliest stages of human development.

Say the word "archaeology," and most people think of dazzling treasures, such as the gold mask buried with King Tutankhamun in Egypt or the gold Inca objects found in the Andes. Archaeologists in Africa do find treasure—but often it is not the kind of treasure you might expect.

In this book, you will learn about discoveries that range from ruined tombs to buried trash heaps. For

∧ This Nubian jewelry is covered in hieroglyphics, a system of writing used by both the Nubians and their neighbors the ancient Egyptians.

archaeologists, such finds are treasures that reveal the story of humankind. They give us a glimpse into the lives of the people who made them.

The search for such artifacts can take people to amazing and dangerous places. While exploring Africa's past, archaeologists have endured freezing temperatures and sizzling heat.

They have braved sandstorms and climbed some of the world's highest sand dunes and dangerous cliffs. Sometimes they must sidestep minefields or avoid poisonous snakes. Their journeys may take them across hundreds of miles of desert with no sign of another person.

The reward comes from finding history—inside caves, on rocks, in buried cities, beneath ruins, and in tombs and graveyards. Archaeologists might be the first people to see or touch an artifact in thousands of years. They might be the first to realize the meaning of already well-known monuments. Even discoveries that seem ordinary can turn out to be important. One such example involves a very unlikely type of treasure indeed: the remains of some bananas—some very, very old bananas.

Food for thought

Bananas have been an important food in tropical Africa for a long time. The fruit made some early African kingdoms wealthy once they learned how to grow large crops. For years, historians thought bananas reached Africa after people on its eastern coast made contact with Southeast Asia,

< A man places his foot next to a footprint made in South Africa 117,000 years ago—one of the earliest traces of modern humans.

V This bronze head depicts a king of the ancient Nigerian city of Ife. It dates to between A.D. 1100 and 1400.

across the Indian Ocean. According to this theory, bananas originated in New Guinea and then spread to Asia. When Asian peoples settled on the island of Madagascar in the first millennium A.D., they took bananas with them. From Madagascar, bananas then reached the African mainland.

In 2000, a discovery in Cameroon suggested an earlier date for bananas' arrival in Africa—around 500 B.C. That surprise made historians rethink their theories. But it was nothing compared to the surprise that was about to follow.

Going bananas in Uganda

In 2001, archaeologist Peter Robertshaw and his team were exploring a small swamp near the site of Munsa, Uganda. Robertshaw was studying the history of the plants that grew in the area. He wanted to find out what changes in plant life revealed about changes in the region's climate and people's way of life. But how do we find out what was growing thousands of years ago? Most vegetable matter rots over such a long time. But traces of pollen sometimes remain to

∧ Stone ruins at Kunduchi in East Africa. The pillar is decorated with imported Chinese plates, evidence of trade with Asia.

tell us about plants. Other useful clues are charred seeds that became hard and dry, perhaps in a bush fire.

Scientists have another way to find out what plants were growing in the past. They look for *phytoliths*, or "plant glass." These hard bits of matter are found in the stems and leaves of many plants. They can be seen only with a microscope, and they survive after the plants themselves have died and decayed. Phytoliths differ in shape and size from plant to plant—great news for archaeologists.

One of Robertshaw's students, Julius Lejju, found buried phytoliths in the swamp. To his astonishment, they turned out to come from ancient bananas. Could bananas have been growing in this unexpected place—and if so, how long ago? The layers of mud above them on the bottom of the swamp had been piling up for more than 5,000 years. If other evidence is found to confirm this discovery, it means that bananas reached Africa much earlier than people thought.

Lejju's discovery could reveal more than just what ancient people ate. It suggests that trade between Africa and Asia, where bananas originated, may have begun much longer ago than generally believed. That might change the way historians see the relationship between ancient Africa and other lands.

Finding the phytoliths was just the beginning. In archaeology, a discovery often raises more questions to answer. How did the bananas get to central Africa from the coast? And how did ancient farmers learn to grow them? It may take many more years of work before we know the answers.

Amazing discoveries

In the following chapters, you will discover other finds that have enlarged our knowledge of ancient Africa and our human story. You will see how fossilized bones and early tools have given us an understanding of the first stages of human development. You will have a chance to examine some of the world's oldest rock paintings and carvings.

You will explore some of the amazing buildings of ancient Africa—including the mysterious ruins of

∧ Vegetation expert Julius Lejju (left) takes a scientific sample from a site in Uganda. Lejju's discovery of parts of ancient bananas may change the way we look at African history.

Great Zimbabwe, a huge stone city that may once have been home to almost 20,000 people, and Jenne-jeno, the oldest city in West Africa. And while exploring the world of the Nubians, you will find out that the ancient Egyptians weren't the only people to build amazing pyramids.

< The incredible workmanship of this ninth-century Nigerian bronze vessel shows that it was made by people with advanced knowledge of metalworking. But we know almost nothing about this society.

Bones, Stones, and Beads

CHAPTER 2

When did prehistoric people learn to think?

Blombos Cave has a spectacular location. It is on a cliff overlooking the Indian Ocean at the southern tip of Africa. But for archaeologists Christopher Henshilwood and Cedric Poggenpoel the real excitement lay not in the view, but within the cave itself. Since 1993, they have found thousands of artifacts, including 28 specialized bone tools that have changed our understanding of human development.

< Archaeologists Christopher Henshilwood and Cedric Poggenpoel search for further evidence of early humans at the excavation in Blombos Cave, South Africa.

EARLY HUMANS
4 MILLION YRS – ca 160,000 YRS B.C.

4 MILLION B.C.   160,000 B.C. 0

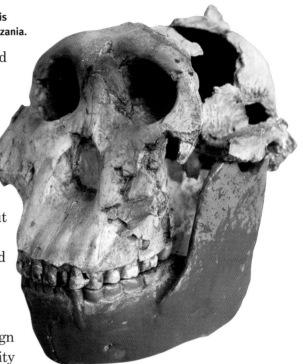

> In 1959, archaeologist Mary Leakey found this 1.75 million-year-old skull in Olduvai Gorge, Tanzania.

Why the excitement? Because crafted bone tools were a major advance for early humans. The widely accepted theory suggested that people did not make such tools until about 45,000 years ago, when they began to leave Africa for other lands. But the tools and other artifacts in Blombos Cave were about 100,000 years old—more than twice as old as most other bone tools found in Africa. Bone tools were being shaped much earlier than scientists had thought.

Scientists see toolmaking as a sign of the development of *hominids* ability to think. The term hominids refers to modern humans, their ancestors, and other creatures that walked upright on two feet. Tool-making requires the ability to think of ways to use materials for practical purposes. The tools in Blombos Cave suggest that the human ability for complex thought developed sooner than anyone had previously believed.

Secrets of the gorge

Everything we know about human origins comes from discoveries in Africa. During the past 60 years, people have found the fossilized bones of various hominids. Some of them date back more than four million years.

Key information has come from Olduvai Gorge in Tanzania, East Africa. Exploration began there by accident. In 1911, a professor named Wilhelm Kattwinkel stumbled into the gorge while he was chasing a rare butterfly. Before climbing back out, he

< Some of the bone artifacts found in Blombos Cave, South Africa

∧ Olduvai Gorge in northern Tanzania is rich in the fossil remains and tools of human ancestors.

picked up some fossils to take home. The fossilized bones turned out to come from extinct animals.

The discovery attracted scientists to the remote gorge over the next decades to hunt for more fossils. They included the anthropologist Louis Leakey and his archaeologist wife, Mary. In July 1959, Mary Leakey found several small pieces of a skull. It was a species of hominid that had never been seen before. It was 1.75 million years old. This important find showed that hominids lived in Africa much earlier than previously known.

Soon afterward, the Leakeys found the remains of another hominid. It had a larger brain and narrower face than other skulls found in Africa. The Leakeys guessed that this hominid had made the tools that they found nearby.

They named it *Homo habilis*—"handy man." *Homo habilis* may be the earliest type of modern human. This hominid lived 2.0 to 1.8 million years ago.

Human origins

Africa continued to reveal secrets about early humans. In the 1970s in Hadar, Ethiopia, Donald Johansen found nearly half of an adult female skeleton he named Lucy. She was about 3.2 million years old and stood just 4 feet (1.2 m) tall. Lucy was an example of an australopithecine, an extinct hominid. The bones of her hip, pelvis, ankle, and feet showed that she walked on two legs rather than four. But no one knows if Lucy was one of our ancient grandmothers.

A nearly complete skeleton of a young *Homo erectus*—"upright man"—

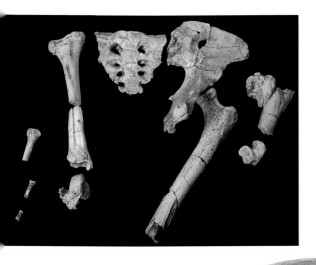

of the puzzle. The evidence we have now suggests that Africa was the origin of several types of hominids, including australopithecines, *Homo erectus,* and *Homo habilis.* About 160,000 years ago, a new species emerged: *Homo sapiens,* or "thinking man." These were anatomically modern humans.

Living with tools

Archaeologists are as interested in how hominids behaved as in how they developed from earlier creatures. They study tools, ornaments, and other objects. Things made from wood or plant fibers are rare. But other objects—made from stones and bones—can still tell their stories.

∧ The hip and pelvic bones of Lucy—the most famous hominid fossil. Her 3.2 million-year-old remains were discovered in Hadar, Ethiopia, in 1974.

was found in Kenya in 1984. Again, he might be a human ancestor. The bones were 1.6 million years old. Other fossilized bones found in Africa show changes over time in the size of early hominids' bones, teeth, and brain.

∧ A skull found at Kabwe, Zambia, in 1921—one of the first human fossils discovered. Its age is uncertain, but it may be 400,000 years old.

In 1925, Raymond Dart was exploring some caves in South Africa. He found animal bones that seemed to be shaped like knives, daggers, and scooping objects. There were so many bones of similar shapes that Dart concluded they were tools. Each had been made for a definite purpose.

Dart's idea was not accepted until more scientists found evidence of toolmaking. At Olduvai Gorge, the Leakeys and others found many shaped stones. They deduced that early hominids had

A great debate

The discoveries in Africa have sparked intense debates among scientists trying to discover the identity of our ancestors. Did humans evolve in one place? Or did they develop in separate regions or even on separate continents? Further finds may provide more pieces

What were they thinking?

Archaeologist Nicholas Toth of Indiana University has spent decades studying ancient tools. He tried a remarkable experiment to learn about how early toolmakers thought. He used a medical technique called Positron Emission Tomography (PET) to take images of his brain while he was copying ancient tools. Toth had radioactive isotopes injected into his brain that would respond to brain activity. As Toth struck flakes from stones, the parts of his brain that were being stimulated showed up on a PET screen. They were the same parts of the brain that have grown most in size over the past 2.5 million years. Toolmaking and the development of human thought are clearly closely linked.

made the tools by using a hard stone as a hammer to chip off some fine-grained rock such as basalt that flakes easily. Using different shaped stones, hominids could cut up dead animals, break bones, or scrape animal hides for clothing. Stone tools are often found near animal bones. At Olduvai Gorge, flaked stones lay near the bones of a hippopotamus—a feast for a group of hominids nearly two million years ago.

By the time people lived in Blombos Cave, they were making more intricate tools. The people who lived there knew how to chip, scrape, and polish bone to produce special tools for various jobs. Double-faced tools with sharp points were used as spear tips for hunting. Awls were used to pierce hides to make holes so they could be sewn to make clothing. Other tools may have been used for fishing, since fish bones were found in the cave.

Arts and crafts?

Some items found in Blombos Cave caused great debate, such as large amounts of ocher, a reddish iron oxide. This material can be mixed with animal fats to make paint. Did the inhabitants use ocher to paint their bodies? The cave also held 41 shells pierced with holes. They are believed to be 75,000 years old. Were they used as beads for a necklace?

Scientists see using body paint and making and wearing jewelry as a sign of a great step forward in the development of the human brain. Is it possible that these early people had the brain and self-awareness to think like modern humans? As more beads are found and dated, experts might learn when this kind of behavior began in Africa—and in the rest of the world.

< This fine hand-ax was found in South Africa and is around 600,000 years old. It was probably made by *Homo erectus*.

Kingdoms on the Nile

CHAPTER 3

What was the secret of the sacred mountain?

Archaeologist Timothy Kendall was frustrated. He had climbed to the top of Jebel Barkal, a steep-sided, flat-topped "sacred mountain" that rose from the plain near the River Nile in Sudan, south of Egypt. From there, he could see inscriptions at the top of the tall, thin rock spire next to the mountain, but he could not make them out. Kendall hoped that they might hold clues about the Nubians, Africans who ruled an empire so powerful that at times it included ancient Egypt.

< A worker reads hieroglyphics in the tomb of Piankhy, a Nubian king who ruled Egypt in the eighth century B.C. The Egyptians called the Nubians Kushites.

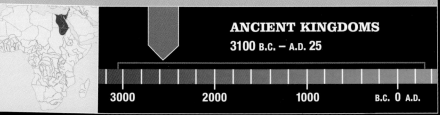

ANCIENT KINGDOMS
3100 B.C. – A.D. 25

3000   2000   1000   B.C. 0 A.D.

∧ A Nubian king receives tribute from Egyptians. Nubia sometimes ruled, and was sometimes ruled by, Egypt.

There was a line of deep holes cut into the cliff that might once have held ropes for a suspension bridge across the gap. For Kendall, however, there was only one way to study the mysterious inscriptions: by climbing the dizzying rock.

Kendall had to be patient. The climb was so difficult that he needed mountaineering lessons. He returned to Jebel Barkal a year later, in 1987. With an experienced climber to help him, he managed to climb the peak. Almost at once, he found something more interesting than the inscriptions.

Bronze nails were poking out of some small, evenly spaced holes in the rock. Kendall had seen a similar group of holes and nails in Egypt. There they had been used to attach sheets of gold

to a surface. Perhaps the nails at Jebel Barkal had been used for the same purpose. If the rock spire at Jebel Barkal had been covered with a sheet of gold, the rising sun each morning would have reflected off it in a golden beam across the desert. That would fit well with the Nubians' worship of the Egyptian sun god, Amun.

Close neighbors

Nubia and Egypt had an uneasy relationship. Sometimes they were at war. At other times, they were part of the same empire. In 2003, a team led by Swiss archaeologist Charles Bonnet uncovered a ditch in an ancient temple in Sudan. It contained seven granite statues of black pharaohs, or kings of Nubia. Two of them were of kings who had ruled both kingdoms.

Bonnet compared the dates on the statues with known historical events. He concluded that the statues had been knocked down when Egyptians invaded Nubia about 593 B.C. The Nubians probably buried the statues in the pit for safekeeping after the attack. Bonnet's discovery opened a new chapter in the story of what may be the world's oldest known monarchy.

Pyramids in Sudan

Archaeologists had started piecing together that story in the early 1900s in northern Sudan. In 1916, a team led by George A. Reisner of Harvard University began investigating pyramids there. Sudan has more pyramids than Egypt. About 1,400 years after the Egyptians stopped using pyramids for royal burials, a Nubian pharaoh, Piye, revived the custom. He reigned from 747 to 716 B.C. Piye ruled both Nubia and Egypt, which he conquered during his reign.

Reisner's team began excavating tombs at el-Kurru, about 10 miles (16 km) from Napata, at

< This bronze mirror has a handle in the form of a woman. It was found on the frontier between Egypt and Nubia at Semna. It was made between 1575 and 1000 B.C.

V A staircase inside Piankhy's tomb. Piankhy was the first Nubian ruler to be buried beneath a pyramid, showing the influence of neighboring Egypt on Nubian culture.

Fancy Meeting You Here...

In 2000, a curator at a museum in Southampton, England, was talking with two Egyptologists when she recalled a statue in the basement. When she got the 27-inch (68-cm) piece, the visitors agreed that it might be important—but they did not realize how important. Experts now believe the 2,700-year-old sculpture depicts Taharqa, the most powerful Nubian king. An old receipt revealed that the statue was a gift from "Mr. Williams" but called the work an "Egyptian figure." Decades ago, experts did not realize that Egypt and Nubia were separate kingdoms. In such cases, an important role of archaeology is to undo the careless mistakes of the past.

one time the Nubian capital. The tombs had been robbed, so any treasure was gone. But they still held rich information for Reisner. He traced how burial customs had changed. The earliest tombs were rough, circular stone structures. The bodies inside were placed on beds in narrow pits. Later tombs were square and topped with small, steep-sided pyramids. Inside the tombs, the bodies were mummified and laid in coffins. This was a typical Egyptian practice.

One surprising find was a grave for 24 horses. They were buried standing up, draped in nets adorned with beads and cowrie shells. Nubians prized their horses highly, and so did other peoples in the region. Reisner found sacrificed animals in human tombs, too.

V **This brick structure located next to a rocky outcrop at Kerma turned out to be a fortress.**

Reisner explored several brick monuments at Kerma, but he did not realize the importance of the site. In the 1960s, archaeologists did more work at Kerma. They found artifacts which showed that Nubia had an advanced political organization in 3300 B.C.—earlier than the first recorded Egyptian king. In 1973, Charles Bonnet led another team that excavated at Kerma.

∧ There are 74 pyramids in the Nubian graveyard at Nuri. Many have crumbled over the centuries. This one is the best preserved.

The ruins showed that it was a large city by 2000 B.C. That makes Kerma, along with early cities in Egypt and Mesopotamia, one of the oldest urban centers in the world.

By the 1970s, archaeologists were also focusing on Napata. This city was the Nubian capital for nearly 1,000 years. Its location near the Egyptian border made it a major center for storing various trade goods for overland shipment. While Egypt sent its cloth and other goods south, the Egyptians prized trade goods from southern Africa: ebony, animal skins, ivory, frankincense, incense, myrrh, and gold.

Royal tombs

About 10 miles (16 km) upstream from Napata stands Nuri, a rich Nubian graveyard. Pyramids mark the royal tombs of 20 Nubian kings and 54 queens. The tombs had chambers cut into the bedrock. They were decorated with scenes from the Egyptian Book of the Dead to help the dead ruler in the afterlife. On the eastern sides of the pyramids, facing the direction of the sunrise, people made offerings to the dead rulers in small chapels.

A great pharaoh

The largest pyramid at Nuri belonged to Taharqa, the greatest Nubian pharaoh. He reigned from 690 to 664 B.C. Taharqa ruled Egypt until the Assyrians invaded and drove him south to Napata. He was known for his great building projects. With these, he hoped to restore Egypt's glory.

Taharqa's pyramid had a sandstone shell enclosing an inner structure. It stood about 260 feet (79 m) high and 171 feet (52 m) on each side. The huge burial chamber had columns carved from the rock and was highly decorated. The floor was deliberately flooded. Taharqa's coffin lay on a raised platform in the center. This is how the Nubians imagined their creator god had emerged from the waters at the beginning of time.

Looters broke into the tomb in the 1800s. But archaeologists still found more than 1,200 *shawabtis*—figures to serve the king after his death. Words inscribed on each figure express its readiness to perform duties in the land of the dead. The shawabtis combined Nubian facial features with the form of an Egyptian mummy.

Political center

Taharqa's pyramid lay within sight of Jebel Barkal, near Napata. Its tip marked the spot where the sun rose on the ancient Egyptian New Year's Day when seen from Jebel Barkal. Beneath the peak stood a temple to Amun, an Egyptian god that the Nubians had adopted as their main god. Jebel Barkal clearly had great spiritual and political meaning.

Timothy Kendall began working in Napata in 1986 with a team from the University of Rome. They found evidence

∧ **This Nubian bronze container has Egyptian images and hieroglyphics.**

of a rich city with temples decorated by fine craftsmen. These temples held sacred statues, objects, and writings on papyrus (a form of paper made from reeds). One find was a large granite statue of Taharqa wearing a cap with two rearing cobras.

The team excavated the temple complex, recorded inscriptions, and carefully noted each carving. They also mapped the ancient city. To do this, they studied photographs and drawings of the individual buildings. They also did an aerial survey. This means they took a series of photographs of the city from an airplane.

A magic snake

Kendall was fascinated by Jebel Barkal, especially after he climbed its peak. He wondered "how a rock formation could have energized an empire." Near the top of the mountain, he found a hollowed-out place. Kendall guessed it once held a statue of Taharqa. He thought that Jebel Barkal might have strengthened the king's political power in some way.

Computers Show What Might Have Been

Computers are useful to archaeologists in many ways, including showing how ruined structures might once have looked. Archaeologists used computers to create an image of the temple at Jebel Barkal, for example. Surveyors measured the temple courtyard, which was buried under 5 feet (1.5 m) of sand. They gathered information from other Nubian temples that are still standing.

Using all this information, they drew up a design. Then they produced an image of the courtyard and temple as those structures might have appeared 2,500 years ago. There is a lot of guesswork involved, however. Images produced in such a way can be helpful, even if there is no way to know exactly how close to real they are.

∧ Sphinxes—lions with human heads—guard the ancient entrance to a temple near the rocky outcrop of Jebel Barkal.

Jebel Barkal's shape may have made it powerful. From the side, it resembles a huge crown; its rock spire stands at the front like a *uraeus*—the rearing cobra emblem worn by the pharaoh on his crown. The cobra was a sign of a protective goddess. Perhaps the Nubians believed that Jebel Barkal helped to guard their capital, Napata.

Jebel Barkal remained the Nubian spiritual center even after 200 B.C.

when Nubian rulers moved south to avoid Egyptian troops. The rulers returned there for ceremonies until their kingdom fell about 200 years later. Nubia did manage to last longer, however, than its old rival Egypt, which was overrun by Persia and then the Greeks, followed by Rome.

Mysterious Stone Ruins

CHAPTER 4

Who built the stone "sacred house"?

One day in 1871, German geologist Karl Mauch was exploring a high plateau between the Limpopo and Zambezi Rivers in southeastern Africa. He found himself staring at a wall of giant stones. Standing up to 32 feet (9.7 m) high, the wall extended 800 feet (244 m) to enclose several smaller walls and two cone-shaped towers. More stone structures stood on a nearby hill, and stone ruins were strewn across the valley below. The complex had been discovered before—but it

< The encircling outer wall of Great Zimbabwe's Great Enclosure rises to a height of 32 feet (9.7 m) from a base that is 17 feet (5.2 m) thick in places.

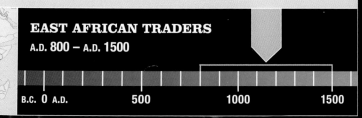

EAST AFRICAN TRADERS
A.D. 800 – A.D. 1500

B.C. 0 A.D.   500   1000   1500

remained a mystery. When Portuguese traders visited the area in 1552, it was already abandoned. Villagers told them about the site they called Zimbabwe. The name meant "stone dwelling" or "house of stone" in the local Shona language. But whose house? What kind of community developed here?

At the time that Mauch visited the ruins, most foreigners still knew little

∧ The central complex at Great Zimbabwe, known as the Great Enclosure. Built at the height of Great Zimbabwe's power in the 14th century, it is the largest single ancient structure south of the Sahara.

about African cultures. He assumed that Africans would not have been able to build such magnificent structures. Mauch thought it was built by people from the Middle East. He guessed that it was Ophir, the legendary capital of King Solomon.

British archaeologist David Randall-MacIver arrived to try to discover who built Great Zimbabwe in 1905. He found his work cut out for him—literally. Treasure-hunters had mixed up layers of soil and discarded pottery and other archaeological clues while removing millions of ounces of gold.

Randall-MacIver studied the walls of the central complex, known as the Great Enclosure. Blocks of granite had been skillfully put together without mortar (a building material that holds bricks or stones together). Randall-MacIver dated the structure to the Middle Ages. But he saw that the curving walls and rounded steps were completely different from Middle Eastern buildings of that time, which were usually square or rectangular.

"African in every detail"

He became convinced that Africans had built the structures. His team sank a trench inside the Great Enclosure and dug up items similar to those still used by the local Shona people. Randall-MacIver also found the remains of mud houses, which he said were "African in every detail."

Another British archaeologist, Gertrude Caton-Thompson, came to study the origins of the site in 1929. After careful excavation of more areas, she confirmed Randall-MacIver's findings. She found that the short walls within the Great Enclosure had once linked huts where people lived. She dug up pottery and soapstone dishes that were African in both style and material. She also found metal objects—bronze and iron spearheads,

Why build a wall?

People build walls for various reasons: to protect against enemies, to mark boundaries, or to keep people in or out. In any case, building a large wall requires many workers—and good organization.

The walls at Great Zimbabwe are an impressive building achievement. Archaeologists have studied them closely for clues about their purpose. They know that the walls were not designed to support roofs. But it is also clear that the openings in the walls would not have provided effective defense against invaders, even though the hilltop location of the earliest walls gave a clear view of potential attackers.

So what purpose did the walls serve? They may have been built to show the rulers' wealth and power, or to protect their privacy. Or people may have prayed there or visited priests. Some areas may have been used for ceremonies to celebrate young people becoming adults.

Evidence for this theory comes from the fact that, after the site was abandoned in the 15th century, local people saw it as a sacred place. But the precise purpose of the stone enclosures remains a mystery—for now.

∧ The double chevron pattern on the outer wall of the Great Enclosure is typical of the area.

iron hoes and nails, copper axes— and tools used for working metals, including gold.

∨ Great Zimbabwe's Hill Complex overlooks the Valley Complex and the Great Enclosure. It contains the earliest stone ruins, some of which date back to the 13th century.

Cattle central

Caton-Thompson's careful study of the layers of remains that had piled up at the site formed a picture of life at Great Zimbabwe over a period of about 1,500 years. Finds at the lowest levels showed that the site was settled by farmers and herders around A.D. 300. They may have moved to the plateau from nearby lowlands to escape the tsetse flies. These flies can carry a disease that kills both domestic animals and people. The plateau had poor soil for farming. But it did have grass for livestock, and stone for building.

Great Zimbabwe—the name given to the whole site—covers almost 1,800 acres (730 ha). Its early inhabitants built round huts from *daga*, a mixture of mud, cow dung, and gravel. Tests showed that the first stone walls were built in the 13th century on the hill. The ruins in the valley are more recent. Archaeologists think the settlement expanded to house a growing population. The city may have held 18,000 people at its peak in the late 1300s, when the walls of the Great Enclosure were built.

By that time, the city had become wealthy—but that posed a question for experts. The poor soil could not support large crops, and the people would have had to buy much of their food from miles away, which would have been expensive.

In the 1960s and 1970s, digging turned up 140,000 pieces of animal bone that might explain Great Zimbabwe's wealth: cattle. The grasslands of the plateau were a good place to rear cattle, which could be traded as well as eaten.

Pots of beads

Other finds revealed another source of growing wealth. One collection of objects found at Great Zimbabwe included coral, brass wire, bronze bells, and copper finger rings, as well as 13th-century ceramics from China and Persia and glassware from Southwest Asia. Such a wide range of finds showed that from the 12th to 15th centuries Great Zimbabwe was part of a trading network that linked the interior with ports on the east coast. In exchange for gold and ivory from central Africa, merchants on the coast traded beads, glassware, cloth, and other goods.

One container found at Great Zimbabwe in

< One of several mysterious half-bird, half-human figures found among the ruins at Great Zimbabwe.

36

1941 held 30,000 glass beads! Gold was also mined in the region beginning in the 13th century.

Other Zimbabwes

Great Zimbabwe is not the only structure of its kind. Many stone ruins are scattered across the region. Some are older, and others are more recent. But the massive size of Great Zimbabwe suggests that it was an economic and political center.

Excavations at other stone-walled settlements have revealed a more

A Point of Pride for the People

Great Zimbabwe is a point of pride for the peoples of the region. Before 1980, Zimbabwe was under British rule. It was called Rhodesia. In 1980, it became an independent nation. The people voted to change the name of their country to Zimbabwe. This may be the only time people have named their country for an archaeological site.

complete picture of Great Zimbabwe. Gold items found at the sites offered a glimpse of the treasure that looters must have taken from Great Zimbabwe. Imported goods found at these sites showed that they were also part of an extensive trade network. They revealed rich royal burials, too. No similar burials have been found at Great Zimbabwe.

Many questions remain. Who built Great Zimbabwe? And why did they abandon it? Scholars still wonder about the meaning of the chevron patterns on the walls and of the mysterious half-bird, half-human figures found among the ruins. Someday archaeology may reveal the answers.

< This solid cone-shaped tower is a striking feature of the Great Enclosure. Its purpose is unknown, but it may have been meant to represent a grain bin.

Show Me a Story

CHAPTER 5

What secrets are revealed in rock art?

French archaeologist Henri Lhote first saw the images scratched and painted onto the rocks at Tassili-n-Ajer in the southeastern Sahara in 1934. The dazzling images stayed with him for 20 years, until he returned on a research expedition. On closer inspection, he was even more excited. With at least 4,000 rock paintings and even more carvings, Tassili is one of the world's greatest collections of prehistoric art. The art dates from around 6000 B.C. to 1200 B.C.

< David Lewis-Williams, a leading expert on African rock art, examines a recently discovered painting in South Africa's Drakensberg Mountains.

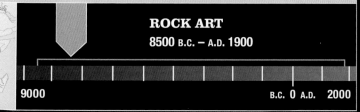

ROCK ART
8500 B.C. – A.D. 1900

9000   B.C. 0 A.D.   2000

For thousands of years, artists around Tassili carved and painted vivid images on rocks. They made paints from sandstone, ocher, zinc oxide (white), and manganese oxide (black). In some areas, preparing ocher had its own ceremony. After heating the ocher, artists ground it up and added animal

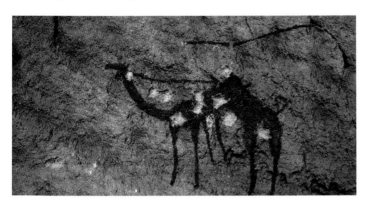

Λ Camels appeared in rock art beginning in the first century B.C. This painting has been vandalized by being repeatedly hit with an object.

fat, egg yolk, or blood to make paint. They carried the paints in containers on their belts and applied them with animal tails, feathers, quills, or bones.

When carving images into the rock, the artists considered how the shadows formed by the passage of the sun would affect their work. They also took into account the angles and curves on the rocks themselves.

A changing land

When Henri Lhote arrived in Tassili-n-Ajer, it was a remote desert region. But around 9,000 years ago, it was a well-watered place where many people and animals lived. Its name means "Plateau of the Rivers." The art there

documents how people adapted as the rivers and lakes shrank and grasslands disappeared. By about 2,000 years ago, the land had become a desert.

Hunting giant buffalo

Lhote began the task of studying the rock art by dividing the works into four main periods, according to the most common styles and subjects. He named the earliest period the "roundhead" era. Its paintings show people with featureless faces and round heads. Hunters chase giant buffalo (now extinct in Africa) as well as ostriches, antelopes, and other wild animals. They use bows, clubs, or axes, and some wear masks. The dates of this period are a subject of heated debate, but were probably 6000 B.C. to 4000 B.C.

The "cattle-herder" period began about 5000 B.C. Scenes of animal herding became common. So did pictures of people farming and doing daily tasks. Archaeologists have found human and cattle bones dating back to 4500 B.C. across the area. These finds confirm that people in the region at the time lived by herding cattle, and were nomads—they had no settled home but moved from place to place.

By about 1200 B.C., horses began to appear in paintings, sometimes

Inside the "Minds" of Ancient Cultures

Excavated objects such as bones and pottery give archaeologists information about how ancient peoples lived their everyday lives. But rock art can give scientists a glimpse into the ways that they thought. How did our ancestors view the world?

Scientists use techniques of a branch of archaeology known as cognitive archaeology to understand the beliefs that drove the behavior of ancient cultures. One way they do this is through studying the symbols people used. A symbol is something that stands for something else. For example, a flag is a symbol of a country. Symbols that reveal people's beliefs and values can be found in their architecture, art, and the objects they made.

pulling chariots. The chariot images suggest that the artists of this "horse" period had contact with eastern Mediterranean peoples because these people used such vehicles. At this time, the Sahara still had enough rainfall to sustain farming and herds of horses, but cattle were becoming more rare.

The "camel" period began around 100 B.C., with images of camels, brought to Africa by the Romans, and other desert animals. They show that the land had become arid as it began turning into the desert it is today.

▽ The desert region of Tassili-n-Ajer was once a lush area with plenty of wildlife. Humans may have lived there as long ago as 6000 B.C. These people left behind thousands of pieces of rock art.

∧ A modern researcher shows how artists carved images into the Saharan rock using stone tools.

Camels had replaced horses as a means of transportation.

As Lhote publicized his findings, people wanted to learn more. They explored new rock-art sites in Africa and found thousands more pictographs (rock paintings) and potroglyphs (rock engravings) After centuries of focusing on European rock art, people began paying more attention to African art. This interest opened new opportunities for archaeologists.

Giraffes in the desert?

A group of giraffes walk along the side of a cliff in Libya. Each stands between 6 and 7 feet (1.8–2.1 m) tall. Photographer David Coulson, an expert on African rock art, first saw the carving in 1998. But the giraffes

had been there for about 7,000 years. They were chiseled with such skill that they seem to be in motion. Even though the area was now desert, the giraffes looked so real that they must have been part of the world where the artist or artists lived. Coulson was not entirely surprised. He had already found giraffes on a rocky outcrop in the desert near Niger's Air Mountains. The two 20-foot (6-m)-tall creatures, known as the Daubous Giraffes, were carved 6,000–9,000 years ago.

Other rocks in Africa's deserts portray crocodiles, antelope, cattle, lions, hippopotamuses, rhinoceroses, and, sometimes, fish and river crabs. Like the rock art at Tassili-n-Ajer, they

How Old Is That Painting?

How do archaeologists date rock art? If the paint contains even minute amounts of organic matter—material that was once living, such as traces of blood or charcoal—they can use *radiocarbon dating*. This method can be used for samples up to 50,000 years old.

Radiocarbon dating detects the amount of carbon 14 in an object. Carbon 14 is a chemical that is present in all living plants and animals. Once they die, it decays at a steady speed. It takes 5,730 years for half of the carbon 14 in plant or animal remains to decay, so scientists can calculate the age of an organism by measuring the amount of carbon 14 it has lost.

Most rock art does not contain organic carbon, however, so dating it is less reliable.

Archaeologists have to rely on *contextual dating*. This is a method of estimating the age of an image from the age of other items found nearby, such as stone tools. But even objects that turn up in the same cave as a piece of art may not be linked to it. They may have been there many years before or after it was created. So experts also look for other clues. These can be found in the condition of the rock or the style of art, which may resemble another work that can be dated.

▽ **This rock painting from Tassili-n-Ajer shows a woman who might be washing someone's hair.**

bear witness to the time when the Sahara was a region of seasonal rains and lush vegetation.

As at Tassili, archaeologists found other evidence to confirm the story told by the rock art. The desert hid bones of giraffes, crocodiles, and fish, as well as pollen and the shells of freshwater snails.

Doors to the spirit world

Rock art is not only a clue to the physical history of a region or a people. Experts in rock art also search the images for any spiritual meanings that might give a clue to how the artists thought or what they believed.

One man who studies rock art is David Lewis-Williams, former director of the Rock Art Institute at

Witwatersrand University in South Africa. Lewis-Williams has spent decades studying the art made by the San people who have lived in southern Africa for 10,000 years. Recently he visited a shallow cave in the Drakensberg Mountains discovered by his colleague Geoff Blundell. They had to squeeze their way past a fallen boulder that had blocked the entrance. The boulder had also protected the

∧ Archaeologist Geoff Blundell traces images from the 20-foot (6-m)-long rock painting he discovered in the foothills of the Drakensberg Mountains of South Africa.

< A delicate detail from a San rock painting, showing a type of large antelope called an eland. Elands are the San people's most sacred animal and often appear in cave paintings.

cave from animals and harsh weather and helped prouon in the treasure inside. Along the cave wall stretched 231 images in a mural 20 feet (6.1 m) long. The San artists had shown humans, animals, and symbols in complex and unusual designs. Lewis-Williams had seen similar images before—but never all in one place.

The mural was so large and complex that it took more than a year to study. Some parts had four layers of paint. Others were so faint that the marks did not show up in photographs. Experts spent weeks making tracings of the images. Then they redrew the images in the laboratory to re-create the original mural.

Humans become animals

Lewis-Williams and Blundell were fascinated by numerous human-animal figures that appeared. The artists had emphasized their animal aspects, such as horns and hooves, and used thin red lines fringed by small white dots to link the figures to other animals. Some images showed people with oddly shaped heads. The archaeologists guessed that perhaps the figures were *shamans*, healers who were in contact with the spirit world. Other pictures seem to show a shaman in a trance as he "becomes" an animal.

Clues from the present

What did the paintings mean? What beliefs inspired their artists? To find out, Lewis-Williams studied the work of German experts Wilhelm Bleek and Lucy Lloyd. They had visited the region in the 1870s and interviewed many San people about their traditions. Some San in the Kalahari Desert still practice rituals in which men go into a trance in order to enter the spirit world. Lewis-Williams became convinced that rock art helped the San connect with the spirit world. He called the rock a "veil between the material and spirit worlds." The images helped the San connect with the spirit world through cracks in the rock that seemed like actual openings into that world.

Harnessing spirits

Lewis-Williams discovered that the San believed the eland, a kind of large antelope, was sacred. They hunted it for food and thought that its spirit lived on after death. Painting its

∧ David Lewis-Williams (left) and Geoff Blundell study the images on a careful copy of the mural.

image was a way to show respect for the animal and its spirit. Some paintings used animal blood, as if the artist wanted the work to contain the eland's very life.

What else will rock art reveal about ancient Africa? Archaeologists continue to study examples of rock art in Zimbabwe, Botswana, Lesotho, Namibia, and elsewhere. The works are very old, dating back hundreds or thousands of years—but they often reflect even older traditions that may go back more than 10,000 years.

City of Surprises

CHAPTER 6

An earring changes our view of the past

Everyone was working quickly at Jenne-jeno in the Niger Delta in West Africa. It was spring 1981. The rainy season was about to begin. That would end digging at the ancient city for the year. Suddenly, a worker held up something shiny. He had dug it up from beneath the city wall built in A.D. 800. Analysis later showed it was a gold earring, the oldest yet found in West Africa. It would help to change our understanding of human

< The magnificent mud-walled Grand Mosque in Jenne, Mali, continues the architectural traditions of the nearby ancient ruined city of Jenne-jeno.

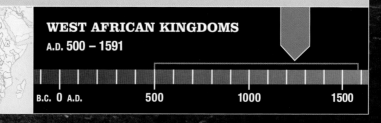

WEST AFRICAN KINGDOMS
A.D. 500 – 1591

B.C. 0 A.D.   500   1000   1500

settlement in the region. There are no gold deposits near Jenne-jeno. That might mean that the city was trading gold by the ninth century. It might also have been wealthy. Fine jewelry is a sign that citizens there enjoyed a comfortable life. Further excavations would show that the city prospered between the 5th and 12th centuries.

Digging the dirt

When Susan and Roderick McIntosh began excavating Jenne-jeno in January 1981, they suspected it held many secrets. Much of the ancient city was buried. But on a visit four years earlier, they had found a range of remains: mud-brick houses, roof tiles, burial urns, skeletons, animal bones, copper bits, and pieces of broken pottery.

∧ A modern inhabitant of Jenne models the gold earring found beneath the ancient city wall.

When they returned to Jenne-jeno, the McIntoshes began to dig in four sites. They hoped that the different layers of remains, or *strata*, would answer many questions about the city: When did people settle there? How did they live? What did they trade? Why did the city decline? How was it connected to the nearby city of Jenne?

Artifacts answered some questions and offered a few surprises. The McIntoshes found charcoal in ancient cooking hearths that radiocarbon testing dated to before 250 B.C. That made Jenne-jeno the oldest known city in West Africa. Experts had thought that Arabs from North Africa built the first cities in West Africa in the 9th century. Clearly, Jenne-jeno was thriving at a much earlier date.

The remains of the city wall provided more evidence of urban life. Scientists dated it to A.D. 400–800. That showed that the society must have been organized enough to bring together the great number of people needed to build such a large structure. The gold earring completed the picture of a wealthy urban settlement.

Layers of life

As they dug down to a depth of 20 feet (6.1 m), the archaeologists found layers marking three major periods: an early settlement from 250 B.C. to A.D. 450; a peak period between 450 and 1100; and a decline from 1200 to 1400. Jenne-jeno had been settled for 1,600 years. West Africa's urban history was twice as long as people once thought.

The first settlers were probably farmers, herders, and fishers. They lived in round homes built from mud and straw. In the upper layers of the

Old Iron Sites

Since African cultures prized iron very highly, it is no surprise that they adopted gods connected with the metal. Among the Yoruba people of Nigeria, for example, Ogun was the god of iron and protector of their kingdom. Ironworkers were respected members of the community because they produced knives, axes, and picks that helped people perform important daily tasks.

By the early 1800s, African ironworkers were producing spears, daggers, and pipes that were widely admired. Tunisian scholar Mohamed el-Tounsy described some iron pipes he saw as "elegant and graceful and shining so brightly they seem to be made of silver." Archaeologists believe that ironmaking technology was introduced to Africa from the Middle East via Egypt.

soil, archaeologists traced changes in the housing. Beginning around the ninth century, mud bricks made of red clay and rice husks became the main building material; they were also used for the city wall. Mud bricks are still used for local building today. By 1100, some houses were rectangular. They reflected the influence of Islamic North Africa, where rectangular buildings were common. Clay also provided material for the large amounts of pottery found at Jenne-jeno. Styles changed over time, but even the early pottery was well made.

The number of houses, along with the variety of artifacts and the vast

▽ A view of the city of Jenne. Like Jenne-jeno it is situated on the floodplains between the Bani and Niger Rivers, which provide a plentiful source of fish.

Learning from Pots and Shards

Various cultures have used clay objects for thousands of years. Baked clay artifacts found at an Upper Paleolithic site in the Czech Republic have been dated back to around 23,000 B.C.

How do archaeologists study pottery that is often broken? First they note the location of each piece, or shard, they find, since that might show how people used it. The surroundings can also help them to date pottery.

As archaeologists classify their finds, they try to put pieces together like a jigsaw puzzle, using the color and shape of the shards as a guide. They also ask questions to help find out more about an object: Where did the material come from? How was the piece shaped and decorated? How was the clay fired? Was the piece made by hand or with a wheel? And what about the texture—fine, medium, or coarse? Is there a rim or handle? What does the base look like?

< A 14th-century terra-cotta container found near Jenne-jeno. Most pottery archaeologists find is broken: it is rare to find a whole pot.

collection of human bones, helped the McIntoshes to estimate the city's population. By A.D. 800, they guessed, about 10,000 people lived there in an area covering about 100 acres (40 ha).

Archaeologists found animal bones and the hulls of African rice, millet, sorghum, and other grains across the city. This showed that residents had a varied diet. In larger homes, people ate grains, beef, catfish and perch, and water birds. Rice was an important food and also a major trading item. Excavation turned up evidence of the oldest known domesticated rice in Africa. It dated back to A.D. 40–400.

With enough food to eat, people had time for crafts and recreation.

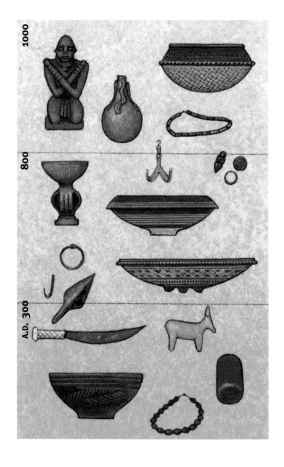

> This diagram shows some important artifacts unearthed at Jenne-jeno and the chronological level in which they were found.

Pieces of clay marked where potters had workshops. Loom weights and spindles revealed areas where weavers once worked. Crucibles for smelting (heating ores to separate out their metals) were a sign that metalworking was well developed. By A.D. 800, craftspeople were making ornaments from brass and copper, and making metals from ores imported from outside the region.

By then, the metalworkers of Jenne-jeno had a long history. The McIntoshes analyzed iron slag deposits (the residue left over from smelting). They discovered that ironworking began with the earliest settlers at the site.

Moving the goods

With a surplus of fish and grain and a location near a major trade route—the Niger River—Jenne-jeno became a busy trade center. Residents sent farm produce, dried and smoked fish, and fish oils to the north. In turn, they imported salt, metal ores, stone, and glass beads.

Around A.D. 750, new overland trade routes across the Sahara linked West Africa with Europe and the Middle East. The new trade contacts also brought a new religion—Islam—to the region.

Abandoned city

In the 1400s, the McIntoshes discovered, people began leaving Jenne-jeno. A new city, Jenne, was founded nearby. Eventually Jenne-jeno was totally abandoned, while Jenne grew into an important Islamic center known for its mosques and religious scholars.

Why did the citizens quit Jenne-jeno? Perhaps religion played a role. Some historians think that, as people adopted Islam, they wanted to leave the city where they had followed the old religion. Or perhaps a plague of some kind drove people away. Further research may provide some answers.

< A terra-cotta horseman found near Jenne-jeno. Similar terra-cotta figures were found in wall cavities in several houses in the city.

Meet an Archaeologist

Rice University professor Susan Keech McIntosh and her fellow professor, Roderick McIntosh, have carried out excavations at Jenne-jeno in Mali, which they discovered was West Africa's oldest known city.

Q When and why did you decide to become an archaeologist?

A I'd always been interested in old things and Greek mythology, and I studied Latin. But it wasn't until I was a college freshman in a survey course in anthropology with a wonderful professor that I found out what I really loved. That decided me and I started studying archaeology and then going for fieldwork.

Q What special challenges have you faced while working in Africa?

A It is, of course, difficult to do a large-scale excavation in a remote place that doesn't have stores that sell things you might be missing or need.

It requires a great deal of planning for supplies for quite a few people and situations. The climate, for people who aren't used to it, is very challenging. It's hot, and you sometimes get ill—but not very often, thankfully. The lack of stores, roads, and planes, and the fact that you have to drive everywhere—it's very challenging but extremely rewarding.

Q What was your most exciting moment so far while working in Africa?

A A lot of fieldwork is very boring. It's just digging and sieving the earth. Most of the hard work of figuring out what it is you've found comes later when you've left the field and

look at all the information you've collected. So for me, my most exciting moment came during one of those times after we had left the field when we got our first radiocarbon dates from the site of Jenne-jeno. We never expected it to be so old. It was at least 500 years older than we thought. Then it kept getting older. Every time we got back more radiocarbon dates from farther down, it got older and older, which was truly thrilling.

Q What work continues today at Jenne-jeno?

A Today there is no active archaeology going on at Jenne-jeno. The main work there now is the excellent work that the cultural mission at Jenne does in preserving the site, introducing it to tourists, and making sure that it is protected from looters.

◘ Are you involved in particular specialty areas within archaeology?

▣ I am. Not only do I study pottery but I study human skeletons buried at Jenne-jeno. They tell us a lot about what kinds of lives people lived—whether they did a lot of hard work or whether they had easy lives, whether they had a lot of cavities. As it turns out, people in Jenne-jeno were pretty healthy.

◘ How do you work with people from other disciplines to study certain findings?

▣ I work very closely with archaeobotanists—people who study plant remains from archaeological sites. That's a very interesting field because you can learn a lot by finding out what kinds of plants were there, including what kinds of plants people ate. I'm very interested in when people domesticated certain plants, especially cereals, and how quickly they became an important part of their diet. Between the hunting and gathering period and the development of agriculture, people's diets really were transformed. I'm interested in studying that transformation and how long it took to occur.

∧ Susan Keech McIntosh and her colleagues at Jenne-jeno, Mali. Her daughter (in pink) peeks out on the left.

◘ How do you prepare for your field trips to Africa?

▣ One thing I do is to lift weights to keep in shape so that I don't hurt myself when lifting buckets out of the pits. One of the main things that we do as a group is to make long lists of items that we need to buy in advance because they're not available in Mali.

◘ How do archaeologists from outside Africa work with local archaeologists?

▣ We work very closely with local archaeologists. In fact, the last two excavations we did both at Jenne-jeno and in Jenne were at the request of Malian archaeologists. They had particular projects that they wanted to do and had raised funds for them. We knew those sites well, so they thought we could contribute to their work and we were very happy to do so. The Malian archaeologists also monitor preservation of the sites. Some of the sites are eroding badly. Others that are very remote are being looted. The Malians know most about the situation and what needs to be done to get information out before the deposits disappear. So we rely on them very much for our collaboration.

Threatened Treasures

CHAPTER 7

How can Africa's cultural heritage be protected and preserved?

From 1999 to 2003, Scott MacEachern was on a rescue mission. Exxon Corporation (now ExxonMobil) planned to dig a 690-mile (1,110-km)-long pipeline from southwest Chad to the Atlantic coast of Cameroon. They asked MacEachern, a professor at Bowdoin University in Maine, to put together a team of African and international experts to save any cultural treasures in the path of the pipeline. The team excavated 309 sites in Cameroon and 163 in Chad, making this the largest archaeological project ever in Central Africa.

< The Nubian Temple of Kalabshah was threatened by the rising waters of Lake Nasser, so UNESCO moved it to its present site near the Aswan Dam in the 1960s.

The team found ironworking sites with smelting furnaces dating back about 2,100 years and stone tools more than 50,000 years old.

This kind of project is sometimes called "rescue archaeology" or, in the United States, cultural resource management. Experts try to locate, document, and save cultural treasures before they are destroyed by building works. A similar project took place in Egypt and Sudan before the Aswan Dam was built on the Nile, creating a lake that flooded a large area. A new

project is scheduled before another dam is built in northern Sudan.

Diverse problems

There are many threats to Africa's archaeological treasures. War and political instability make some places too dangerous for archaeologists. Other sites are extremely remote. A number of countries do not have money to fund research, museums, and exhibits, or programs to train archaeologists. Lack of money also makes it hard to protect sites from environmental threats such as floods. Since 1981, for example, about 10 percent of the deposits at the ancient city of Jenne-jeno have been lost due to wind and water wearing away the surface of the soil.

Looting is also common. At Jenne-jeno, poor farmers have dug up terra-cotta statues and other items to sell to dealers and collectors. Looting has affected an estimated 80 to 90 percent of all archaeological sites in Africa. It always damages a site, often seriously. In about 2 percent of cases, looting completely destroys the historical importance of a site.

Because of its location, rock art is vulnerable to many types of damage. The surfaces on which it is created flake over time. Animals damage it when they enter caves for shelter and rub against the walls. Rain and other elements can wash away the surfaces

‹ Archaeologists excavate a site found during the construction of the Exxon pipeline in Central Africa to evaluate its importance.

of paintings. Conservationists can apply sealing materials—but that does not prevent looting. By 1999, about 40 percent of the rock carvings and 10 percent of the rock paintings in Africa had been damaged or stolen.

What can be done?

International organizations have acted to protect cultural treasures. In 1970, UNESCO, the cultural branch of the United Nations, passed a convention to encourage nations to help each other to tackle the illegal trade in antiquities (valuable ancient artifacts). UNESCO has also made a list of World Heritage Sites, including several in Africa. Listed sites receive international recognition, funding, and support. Laws made by individual nations also help. Several

∧ In 1995, the Getty Conservation Institute carried out conservation work at Laetoli in Tanzania, the site of the oldest known hominid footprints.

African countries have passed tough laws to punish those who harm archaeological sites and artifacts.

The Trust for African Art is an organization set up in 1996 to protect, restore, and make copies of rock art. Artists have spent hours crouching in caves or perched on ledges to make copies. Efforts to preserve rock art began many years ago. In 1954, a team of artists in Tassili-n-Ajer in the Sahara endured wind, heat, and cold to trace paintings. They produced 800 copies that can now be seen around the world. Through efforts like these, we can appreciate and study these works for many years to come.

The Years Ahead

For decades, most archaeology in Africa has been carried out by Europeans or Americans. Today, more local archaeologists are learning to uncover their past and protect cultural treasures. People from 16 sub-Saharan countries attended the Africa 2009 Rock Art Conservation course in Namibia in July 2006. It was sponsored by the National Museums of Namibia, UNESCO, and the National Heritage Board of Sweden. Participants learned how to document and preserve art, and how to present it to the public.

Archaeologist Roderick McIntosh noted, "Despite severe financial crises, several African nations have a well-trained second generation of archaeologists trained in Africa." He hopes that this new generation will convince their governments to fund field research and museums and pass laws that protect Africa's past. They can also help to show other Africans why archaeology is important. Says McIntosh, "If they succeed, not only will they have won a victory for Africa, but they will have set an example for the rest of the world."

∧ Archaeologists take soil samples in Chad, hoping to find artifacts or other traces of human occupation.

Glossary

anthropology – the study of humans and their ancestors in relation to their physical, social, and cultural development

antiquities – relics or artifacts from ancient times

archaeologist – a person who studies the material remains of an ancient culture

artifact – any object changed by humans, especially a tool, weapon, or ornament of archaeological interest

ca – abbrievation for "circa," meaning "about" and used to indicate a date that is approximate

cemetery – a place where a number of dead bodies are buried

circa – about; used to indicate a date that is approximate, and abbreviated as ca

conservation – archaeological work that aims to protect ancient objects or buildings from further damage

contextual dating – a way of dating an object by comparing its age with that of the objects found near it

crucible – a container used for heating metals at high temperatures

excavation – an archaeological dig

fossil – the remains of an organism (such as a plant, animal, or human) that lived in earlier times, preserved in Earth's crust

hominid – the family of primates that includes modern humans, their ancestors, and related forms that walked upright on two feet

legendary – relating to a story that is well known but probably only partly true, or perhaps not true at all

looter – robber; person who steals objects of value

Middle Ages – the period of European history from about A.D. 500 to about 1500

mortar – a building material, like cement, that hardens to hold objects together

ocher – an iron ore, reddish or yellow in color, often used as a pigment to make paint

paleontology – the study of different forms of life that existed in the past, based on examining their bones or fossils

petroglyph – carvings on stone made during prehistoric times

phytolith – hard bits of microscopic matter found in the stems and leaves of certain plants that survive after plants have died and decayed

pictograph – signs or symbols drawn or painted on stone during prehistoric times

radiocarbon dating – a method of dating an object based on measuring the amount of the chemical carbon 14 that it contains

restoration – the process of repairing old objects and buildings to bring them as close as possible to their original state

ritual – repeated practice that relates to specific ceremonies

shaman – a person who performs rituals, magic, and spells

smelting – the process of melting ores to separate out the different metals

sorghum – a plant that is grown for food as a source of grain and syrup

terra-cotta – a brownish-red clay used for making pottery

tomb – a place where a dead body is kept

tsetse fly – a type of fly that can transmit sleeping sickness and other dangerous infections to people and domestic animals

Bibliography

Books

Bordaz, Jacques. *Tools of the Old and New Stone Age*. New York: Natural History Press, 1970.

Forte, Maurizio. *Virtual Archaeology: Re-Creating Ancient Worlds*. New York: Harry N. Abrams, 1997.

Leakey, Mary D. *Olduvai Gorge*. Cambridge: Cambridge University Press, 1971.

Welsby, Derek A. *The Kingdom of Kush*. Princeton, N.J.: Markus-Weiner Publishers, 1996.

Articles

Coulson, David. "Preserving Sahara's Prehistoric Art." NATIONAL GEOGRAPHIC (September 1999): 82–89.

Kendall, Timothy. "Kingdom of Kush." NATIONAL GEOGRAPHIC (November 1990): 96–125.

Lhote, Henri. "Oasis of Art in the Sahara." NATIONAL GEOGRAPHIC (August 1987): 181–91.

McIntosh, Susan Keech, and Roderick McIntosh. "Finding West Africa's Oldest City." NATIONAL GEOGRAPHIC (September 1982): 396–418.

Further Reading

Bessire, Mark. *Great Zimbabwe*. New York: Franklin Watts, 1999.

Haskins, Jim. *African Beginnings*. New York: Amistad, 1993.

Moloney, Norah. *The Young Oxford Book of Archaeology*. New York: Oxford University Press, 1997.

Parker, Linda. *The San of Africa*. Minneapolis: Lerner Publications, 2002.

Poynter, Margaret. *The Leakeys: Uncovering the Origins of Humankind*. Springfield, N.J.: Enslow Publishers, 1997.

On the Web

Archaeology in ancient Nubia
http://www.dignubia.org/sitecredits/

Metropolitan Museum of Art: African rock art
http://www.metmuseum.org/toah/hd/sroc/hd_sroc.htm

University of Chicago's "Vanished Kingdoms of the Nile"
http://oi.uchicago.edu/OI/PROJ/NUB/NUBX92/NUBX92_brochure.html

UNESCO World Heritage Sites
http://whc.unesco.org/pg.cfm?cid=31

Index

< A Kerma ware pottery beaker from Sudan. This fine pot was made by hand without using a wheel. It dates from between 1750 B.C. and 1550 B.C.

About the Author

VICTORIA SHERROW is a veteran author of both fiction and nonfiction for young readers. She has written on diverse topics, including endangered animals, the Great Depression, medical ethics, and the *Titanic*. Her work has appeared on the Best Books for the Teenage and outstanding trade books for science and social studies lists. This is her first book for National Geographic. Ms. Sherrow received her B.S. and M.S. degrees from the Ohio State University.

About the Consultant

JAMES DENBOW is an Associate Professor at the University of Texas at Austin, specializing in the later Stone Age and Iron Age periods. He set up an antiquities program for the Botswana government, running it from 1980 to 1986. He has carried out excavations at sites in the Kalahari Desert and Okavango Delta for more than 20 years. Since 1987, he has also conducted archaeological research in the Republic of Congo.

Sources for Quotations

Page 30: Kendall, Timothy. "Kingdom of Kush." NATIONAL GEOGRAPHIC, November 1990, pp. 96-125.
Page 34: Connah, Graham. *African Civilizations: An Archaeological Perspective*. 2nd edition. Cambridge: Cambridge University Press, 2001.
Page 45: Lewis-Williams, David. "Paintings of the Spirit." NATIONAL GEOGRAPHIC, February 2001, pp. 118-125.

Page 49:"Les Routes de Fer en Afrique" (The Iron Roads in Africa). Paris: UNESCO, 2000.
Page 58: McIntosh, Roderick. "Africa's Storied Past." *Archaeological Institute of America*, Volume 52, Number 3, May/June 1999.

Copyright © 2007 National Geographic Society
Published by the National Geographic Society.

All rights reserved. Reproduction of the whole or any
part of the contents without written permission from
the National Geographic Society is strictly prohibited.
For information about special discounts for bulk
purchases, contact National Geographic Special Sales:
ngspecsales@ngs.org

One of the world's largest nonprofit
scientific and educational organizations, the
National Geographic Society was founded in
1888 "for the increase and diffusion of
geographic knowledge." Fulfilling this
mission, the Society educates and inspires millions
every day through its magazines, books, television
programs, videos, maps and atlases, research grants,
the National Geographic Bee, teacher workshops, and
innovative classroom materials. The Society is
supported through membership dues, charitable gifts,
and income from the sale of its educational products.
This support is vital to National Geographic's mission
to increase global understanding and promote
conservation of our planet through exploration,
research, and education.

For more information, please call 1-800-NGS-LINE
(647-5463) or write to the following address:

National Geographic Society
1145 17th Street N.W.
Washington, D.C. 20036-4688
U.S.A.

Visit the Society's Web site:
www.nationalgeographic.com

Library of Congress Cataloging-in-Publication Data
available upon request
    Hardcover ISBN-10: 0-7922-5384-1
        ISBN-13: 978-0-7922-5384-6
    Library Edition ISBN-10: 0-7922-5399-X
        ISBN-13: 978-0-7922-5399-0

Printed in Mexico

Series design by Jim Hiscott
The body text is set in Century Schoolbook
The display text is set in Helvetica Neue, Clarendon

National Geographic Society

John M. Fahey, Jr., *President and Chief Executive
Officer;* Gilbert M. Grosvenor, *Chairman of the Board;*
Nina D. Hoffman, *Executive Vice President, President
of Book Publishing Group*

Staff for This Book

Nancy Laties Feresten, *Vice President, Editor-in-Chief
of Children's Books*
Virginia Ann Koeth, *Project Editor*
Bea Jackson, *Director of Design and Illustration*
Lori Epstein, Greta Arnold, National Geographic Image
Sales, *Illustrations Editors*
Jean Cantu, *Illustrations Specialist*
Carl Mehler, *Director of Maps*

Priyanka Lamichhane, *Assistant Editor*
R. Gary Colbert, *Production Director*
Lewis R. Bassford, *Production Manager*
Maryclare Tracy, Nicole Elliott, *Manufacturing
Managers*

For the Brown Reference Group, plc

Tim Cooke, *Managing Editor*
Emily Hill, *Project Editor*
Alan Gooch, *Book Designer*
Becky Cox, *Picture Manager*

Photo Credits

Front cover: © Courtesy Entwistle Gallery, London/
Werner Forman Archive; Spine: © J. Norman
Reid/Shutterstock; Back cover: © Werner Forman
Archive; Figure: © Lakis Fourouklas/Shutterstock.com

NGIC = National Geographic Image Collection 1,
© Werner Forman Archive; 2–3, © Robert Aberman/
Werner Forman Archive; 4, © Werner Forman Archive;
6, © J. Norman Reid/Shutterstock; 8, © Nonofho
Mathibidi, National Museum of Botswana; 10 left,
© Pascal Goetgheluck/Science Photo Library; 10 right,
© Archaeological Museum, Khartoum, Sudan/Werner
Forman Archive; 11, © Courtesy Entwistle Gallery,
London/Werner Forman Archive; 12–13, © Michael
Freeman/Corbis; 14, © Werner Forman Archive; 15 top,
© Kenneth Garrett/NGIC; 15 bottom, © British
Museum, London/Werner Forman; 16, © Werner
Forman Archive; 17 top, © Professor Peter Robertshaw;
17 bottom, © Hutchison/Eye Ubiquitous; 18–19,
© Kenneth Garrett/NGIC; 20 top, © Tanzania National
Museum, Dar es Salaam/Werner Forman Archive;
20 bottom, © Kenneth Garrett/NGIC; 21 top,
© Hutchison/Eye Ubiquitous; 22 up, © Science Photo
Library; 22 bottom, © DK Limited/Corbis; 23,
© Akg-Images; 24–25, © Randy Olson/NGIC; 26,
© James M. Gurney/NGIC; 27 up, © Archaeological
Museum, Khartoum, Sudan /NGIC; 27 bottom,
© Randy Olson/NGIC; 28, © Randy Olson/NGIC;
29, © Randy Olson/NGIC; 30, © Archaeological
Museum, Khartoum, Sudan/NGIC; 31, © Jonathan
Blair/NGIC; 32–33, © James L. Stanfield/NGIC; 34,
© Ariadne Van Zandbergen/FLPA; 35 top, © James L.
Stanfield/NGIC; 35 bottom, © Deb Winters/Hutchison/
Eye Ubiquitous; 36, © Private Collection, Heini
Schneebel/Bridgeman Art Library; 37, © Werner
Forman Archive; 38–39, © Kenneth Garrett/NGIC; 40,
© David Coulson; 41, © Thomas J. Abercombe/NGIC;
42, © David Coulson; 43, © David Coulson; 44 top,
© Kenneth Garrett/NGIC; 44 bottom, © Kenneth
Garrett/NGIC; 45, © Kenneth Garrett/NGIC; 46–47,
© Sarah Leen/NGIC; 48, © Michael Kirtley; 49, © Remi
Banali/NGIC; 50 top, © Royal Museum of Central
African Art, Tervuren/Werner Forman Archive; 50
bottom, © NGIC; 51, © Courtesy Entwistle Gallery,
London/Werner Forman Archive; 52, 53, © Susan
Keech McIntosh; 54–55, © Bojan Breceij/ Corbis; 56,
© Scott MacEachern; 57, © Kenneth Garrett/NGIC; 58,
© Scott MacEachern.

Front cover: The head of an *oba*, or king of Benin
Page 1 and back cover: A carved hippopotamus from
Democratic Republic of the Congo
Pages 2–3: The Great Enclosure at Great Zimbabwe